Dancing With My Shadow

Selected Poems

Enjoy this journey !

Warren

Warren K. Olson

authorHOUSE®

AuthorHouse™
1663 Liberty Drive
Bloomington, IN 47403
www.authorhouse.com
Phone: 1-800-839-8640

First published by AuthorHouse 12/22/2009

ISBN: 978-1-4490-4835-8 (sc)

Printed in the United States of America
Bloomington, Indiana

This book is printed on acid-free paper.

Introduction

First and foremost, thank you for your interest in *Dancing with my Shadow*.

This book is a compilation of poems and essays about daydreams, nightmares, love and loss; many of the entries cover more than one of these subject matters within their content. Some of the subjects are from my early teens, and all are from a mind of an explosive passion for life; passion from the moment experienced at the time!

The loss of someone I loved so very much is reflected in much of my later work. However, finding another *special* person after that loss is also part of what you will read. So, like the Phoenix, from devastation comes growth. And so, Karen, I miss you terribly; and to that special person, you make my heart smile.

Dear reader, I hope you enjoy your walk through the mind of an everyday man. My greatest wish is that you find some value in these words. If one line in one poem brings back a memory or touches your heart, then my writing (and sharing) was not in vain.

Warren K.Olson
September, 2009
Morris, IL

Foreword

Magic exists.

And if you don't look carefully, it is so easy to miss it. Like many of those who have gone before us, it is our natural propensity to be busy. We're busy with work. We're busy with school. We're busy with living. We don't have time for the silly things like magic. After all... we're busy!

Yet magic persists.

The wide-eyed wonder of a child who for the first time realizes she can walk - magic! That which inspires us to befriend, and lets another be our friend - again – magic! Even the pain and bitterness that can come from tragedy are mystical to those with the eyes to see their transformational power.

Perhaps one of the strongest of our spells is the magic we weave when we arrange letters on a page to create the pictures in our minds we call thoughts. After all, in the end analysis, the spell is created of only ink and paper. Yet, this enchanted code creates the visions we see, and the emotion we feel, when we read good writing.

So, as you read these pages, ponder their magic. It is possible you may find some words that speak to your own life. In fact, it is entirely possible you may read and have a reaction that is absolutely visceral. Such reaction could not exist but for magic. So read, considering the magic existing all around you, each and every day.

T. Brent Newman

Dedication

To all the people I've met,
to all the places I've visited,
and to the memories they created.

To the "One woman in time"

To T. Brent Newman, for his patience, confidence, and kindness;
without him this book would still be but a dream. Thank you, dear
friend!

Life is a process, not an event,
... a journey, not a destination

Life

$100 a Month

$100 a month, radio, no TV.
A dirty efficiency kitchenette; couch, easy chair, coffee table, lamp.
The bedroom, linens furnished, is separated from the rest of the place by
a shower curtain that matches the shower curtain around the tub;
$100 a month.

French doors that open to an creaky balcony,
and a view of the valley and stream below.
Stairs, nearly as steep as a ladder, creak more than the balcony.
A closet and dresser that will hold more clothes than I have with me,
and with the odor of fresh cedar; all for
$100 a month.

This place has privacy, a clean spot to park my car
and outlets enough for my stereo and guitar.
What the hell, I'll only be here late in the night and on Sundays,
for two months.

My first place! A paradise in the prairie (in knotty pine)
complete with a charcoal grill!
5 miles from town and a hundred miles from nowhere.
This will be a good place to play some rock-n-roll,
drink 3.2% beer, and strum a Hank Williams song when I'm blue.

The good in me left with my innocence;
I'm running to something and not away from anything.
I'm starting a job that I may not be able to handle,
a life that scares the shit out of me,
facing the demons of my past,
and those of my future!

It's getting dark now and the lamp will bring some comfort
until I can find something more than farm news on the radio.
For some reason it seems cold in here and I feel like I could puke!
A whole new world,
all for $100 a month!

3

Almond Eyes

Dark hair frames her face;
eyebrows arch as her eyes rise to meet mine.
Leaving two bodies close within love's space,
dark hair under starlit skies.

Dark almond – shaped eyes that glisten;
eyes that smile an internal smile,
causing a rapid heart to hasten,
to hold love near for a while.

Dark skin that reflects the moonlight,
creating cream-colored lines as the moon shines;
lighting a path for a lover to trace in the night...
to savor all that he finds.

A soft voice that gets softer with a whisper,
with a sigh as he moves along her path.
A body that trembles with involuntary gestures,
a swelling of previously unfelt emotion, one she dreams will last.

The silence of the night is broken
by the sound of breathing, and carried on love's wind.
The two lay together listening to words unspoken,
each praying this time never ends

Ancient Ones

The spirits of the Ancient Ones visit this land often. The misty apparitions walk
the river bluffs,
stopping now and then to shade their saddened eyes with their hands as they stare
longingly onto the vast plains before them.

The plains have changed from tallgrass to wheat, and are noticeably void of
wild game.

Once this open space stretched for hundreds of miles, now it is carved into
manicured
homesteads and symmetrical fields.

The older children of the Ancient Ones roamed the plains freely until deceit
robbed them of that freedom; that deceit still holds them on the least
inhabitable places within their universe.

The Ancient Ones shake their heads in sorrow and weep openly over the
collective heart of their children's children that is cupped in ancient hands.
They turn and walk slowly into the place of their dreams, and disappear
.........................in the manicured present.

Big Simon

Big Simon is an Indian, lives at the end of the reservation;
he lives here in a wall-less prison
as does the rest of the Sioux Nation.

Simon does not have a job, for here there is very little to do,
except to fish - when they're biting, and hunt - when they're running,
and trust the BIA will take care of you.

Simon tries to supplement his government checks when he's able;
but he did more so in the distant past;
part for his pride....
then just to put more food on the table.

He helped raise four boys, fought in the Asian jungle, and ran
cattle for some of his life;
and early on he took to drinking, cost him his boys and his wife.

He spends most of the time telling old stories and trying to
get a ride into town. The stories regale in a past of fake glories
and a careful listener can see the false crown.

Two pair of jeans, three shirts, all faded, not a lot to
show for a lifetime it seems; and that which is left the man has degraded
leaving him with only his *self-broken* dreams.

Big Simon can't change and the system won't let him, and so he lives
with life's greatest fears. Just another poor Indian stuck on the reservation,
riding the trail of his own Trail Of Tears.

Bittersweet Tropic

Romance in the tropics,
browned bodies holding on to each other,
and to the moment.

It's hard to tell the difference between the
sounds of the surf,
and that of two hearts rapidly beating.

Salt water spray, or the salty taste of sweat;
music composed by the birds,
or a chorus within two minds?

Soft, sand covered dark curves,
damp black hair to the waist,
and a smile that hides time's passing.

The heat of passion confused with that of the sun;
no sleep, as night turns too quickly into day.
and one hears the jets leave hourly,
so you must hold tight to this place...to this time.

The bittersweet scenes of romance in the tropics,
...........as you dance to the waves night music.

Bobby

You see him walking the streets from morning to night,
taking time off for his part-time jobs.
He shuffles along, cigarette in tight lips,
dressed in old faded shirt and pants,
wearing socks with broken sandals.

He stops every couple of blocks and rests on the street side benches,
starring into store windows at items he will never own.
The passersby give indignant glances in his direction as he
smiles and nods a shy hello;
they are not so much embarrassed for
him as they are for themselves,
for he treats their indignation
with simple dignity.

He knows he is not one of them,
he has never been.
He has given up on trying to understand why he is so different,
why his life is not like theirs;
it's just always been that way.

Its dusk now and the street lights have come on.
He lights another cigarette as he rises from the bench,
and nods an evening hello to a *perfect* young couple heading
for a local bar; they barely tolerate his gesture;
and he shuffles-off on his rounds.......with dignity!

Cane

The cane fields are ready for harvesting,
the tall blossoms sway in the wind
and the workers watch from the villages
waiting for the harvest to begin.

Its hard and hot work cutting cane,
and you can see by the cuts on their hands
that a lifetime of working the fields takes a toll
as you count the scars on every cane man.

The weather's been good for the cane this year,
there will be plenty of work in the fields.
The men wait and sharpen their blades; it's a sharp
blade and strong back that causes the cane to yield.

They'll work until all the cane is in,
sweating in the mid-day sun,
and swinging the blade with their bodies bent
until the harvest is done.

Each making just enough to see them through,
feeding the family is the reason,
then languishing and looking for part-time work
as they await the blossoms of a new cane season.

Caribe

It's late, and a few stragglers walk hand-in-hand on the beach.
Wispy clouds play tag with the moon and the sand is cool under my feet.
A warm yet cooling wind is blowing in and
small waves tenderly kiss the shore.
As the moonlight dances upon the water,
I know I've been here before.

A school of jellyfish surround the creaking dock,
And the old faded wooden fishing boats gently bob and rock.
A spiny sea urchin rolls in to the end of a wave, landing next to a boat oar,
And as the moonlight shimmers across the water,
I know I've been here before.

Far out on the horizon, the soft lights of a tour ship
blend with that of the stars,
And the quiet of the night is broken by tourists
returning from beach-side bars.
But the silence of the evening soon returns to that of yore;
And as the moonlight plays upon the water,
I know I've been here before.

I walk the beach and stare in to now darkened beach hotels;
on the way back, I stop to wade in to collect some broken sea shells.
I stack them in a pyramidal form along the lapping shore,
And as the moonlight kisses the shells goodnight,
I know I've been here before.

Its 2:00 a.m. by the time I leave the beach to sit on large beach rocks,
within a few minutes I'm back to my shack stretched out in the old hammock.
I close my mind and listen to the beauty as I knock on nature's door,
And as the moonlight fades within my closing eyes,
I know I've been here before.

Charlotte

A beautiful girl with dark hair, dark eyes, and a friend of mine,
has aged through poverty, abuse, and alcohol over time.

When young she was so filled with promise and dreams,
but 40 long years on the reservation has torn life's cloak at the seams.

Too many nights, with too many men, has trapped her deeply within;
being poor hasn't helped, her self-reliance is gone, and addiction has set in.

No time for her God, no time for her kids, no husband to play a role
as she goes through her life in a haze and a blur, for little is left of her soul.

So she will spend the rest of her time on bad men and cheap wine,
continuing to search her life-skies for something she will never find.

And Charlotte's history of failures in life is her lament,
a heart that is saddened and hollow, from a life so foolishly spent.

They will find her in Montana's winter, frozen by the side of the road,
and few will morn her passing except a white man, a friend of old.

Clearing the Cobwebs

It is time to clear the cobwebs from my mind,
they are but dusty gatherings
of random memories and thoughts of a lifetime.
The cobwebs are heavily laden with fragmented pieces and bits and,
although they served me well, they no longer fit.

The person I have become with age is a person of a "new day",
and now it's time for this seldom used collection to be swept away.
The cobwebs cling to the corners of my memory, having grown longer
with passing time; now I look forward to a cobweb-free mind.

The cleaning and clearing will take some time, but I know I must try
to reach a place of relative comfort within my mind's eye.
The process has started, although the shadows of time have
strengthened each web,
leaving me to direct (with wisdom imparted),
that which is needed to put the cobwebs to bed.

Convenient Lie

Star-crossed lovers dining by soft lights,
while across the room another couple sits in quiet desperation,
the lovers thinking only of this night,
and the others in silent anticipation.

Now, past love, they live a life of what is *right*,
hiding under a cloak which , thankfully,
serves as their foundation.

Children, grown and gone, and maybe grandkids soon,
they smile into the empty night to hide their graying gloom.
That of a loveless life, one of no passion,
a structured life that time alone has fashioned.

For time together is all that is left,
a short walk under a make-believe sun, under clear sky.
For that time is a convenient gift...
as they live a convenient lie!

Coyote

She moves across the prairie under moonlight,
weaving a meandering trail through the night
on a hunt that may last past daybreak,
searching for a meal that she, and hunger, deems just right.

She is thin, and her fur has been mottled by age.
She darts in and out of small ravines, then to a path along the stream,
circling the stand of white pines that sit on the small butte,
the pines in the night look like silhouettes in a dream.

This old coyote has survived the hunters the past 3 or 4 years,
and perhaps many more years than I've known;
and I watch from the line shack's small porch and I wonder,
.........how much longer can she call this place home?

Darkskin Beauty

Skin so dark it shines in the moonlight,
yet casts a seductive shadow at each curve;
dark skin, with the scent of the Gardens of Babylon
coupled with soft coconut oil.
Her smile is one of truth and holds a beauty of its own
hiding years of hunger, island sadness, lost loves,
and constant island toil.

She of rapid-fire speech in excitement,
can speak but with a whisper in the dark,
and within the whispers a promise,
a promise from the heart.
Her tight black hair is short cropped, and even within
the dark, salty, sweaty darkness of lovemaking, it retains its place,
until the movement of hands in passion arranges it to frame her face.

She is a dreamer, a schemer, full of island wants;
a man who will work and not beat her;
But she knows my ten days will pass in a hurry, and she'll be left alone,
alone with her dreams and schemes, and so much alone with her fear.
So she swears she will wait until my quickest return,
and hopes I will then take her home.

She is one of forbidden love, this darkskin beauty,

and oh my parents would freak,

to find white legs and dark legs entwined in the moonlight on a secluded beach.

But, colors are no match for love and passion a

s we each seek a place in our minds,

an island visitor and a darkskin beauty

making the best of life's short time.

So we laugh, love and cry thru' ten days in the sun,

young hearts filled with hope,

But we know in those hearts that the end will come

as we hold on thru the nights;

each silently praying without ever saying that which is in our soul,

the end will come for this darkskin beauty on the tenth day's evening flight.

Death Wagon / Little Ed

The death wagon rolls up to the old shack in the Pines after crossing the hardpan
bottom of the shallow stream;
there to meet two he left behind as he passed
into a forever winter's dream.

He worked his hand at everything, trapping, and ranching,
and panning for gold;
going through his life as optimistic as spring,
always leaving his life's story untold.

Never did accomplish much and he left very little behind.
Yes, he kept his horse,
his freedom, and much to himself,
as the way led into his life's decline.

A hard-working old fool, he'd help where he could,
for pay, whiskey, or food;
and he thought his life was one of no good
and never let his feelings protrude.

But we all knew the good that was kept in the man,
he shared that with all who would partake;
showing quiet kindness and wisdom to most,
while thinking he was one of nature's mistakes.

The death wagon moves up the Canyon in light
carrying the stiffened remains of a life,
bones broken to make his body lay flat,
as he moves into a peaceful and permanent night.

Dim Light's Cast

Shadows playing against the wall from a dim light's cast,
within the memory replays the story of a love meant to last.
Of touch and sounds and feelings true, two hearts that beat as one,
now within the haze of the dim light's cast the collective spirits' gone.

Now through the days of endless time a shadow walks alone,
and a heart once filled is empty now as it stands on its' own;
and still within a fading memory silhouettes' from the past
play against memory's wall, from a dim light's cast.

Distant Voices

Do not expect me to stay, for the wind calls me,
the sound of a distant thunder beckons my time,
echoes in the valleys from whispers on a mountain top,
all distant voices playing in my mind.

The sounds of the ocean as the waves kiss the shore,
raindrops caressing tropical leafs ,leaving them to bend,
and the feeling of sand under my feet
as my movements mimic those of the wind.

The sunrise on the horizon, moonlight reflecting the night,
wispy clouds in darkness and daylight,
traversing the heavens at will, as they choose,
and to the minds-eye a profound delight.

No, do not expect to stay for life calls me
to witness all that has been left for this time,
for I must answer that which has called,
….those distant voices whisper in my mind.

Dreams

Dreams, many tied to the past.
Dreams, many seeing into the future.
All keeping me balanced with their faded cast,
and all serving as my minds teacher.

Dreams filled with wants, a few filled with regrets,
giving my life direction, giving my life meaning.
Dreams, some remote, some clear and on-target
aiding my memory, helping me plan; all this from dreaming.

The dreams sometimes blend in the night,
causing confusion within a sleeping mind,
and a struggle ensues to hold separate dreams tight,
for each is too important to leave behind!

Time has told, and time will tell;
only the perception of the future is uncertain,
leaving me subconsciously in- charge, to quell
the closing tight of life's final dream curtain.

Dream Visitors

People fading in and out of my dreams,
faceless and yet I know them.
Most leave a message requiring interpretation,
while others are more blunt it seems.

Their movements in a sleeping mind are like curtains blowing in the breeze;
mentally hard to catch, harder still to hold,
as my mind struggles to please.

They all have a purpose for their visit but sometimes I don't understand
why they bother a restless yet sleeping mind.
Still they come and go at will, just as they have throughout my time.

So I'm forced to accept their interruptions, to listen to messages ill-defined,
and to replay the moments and their movements until dawn
when morning's light reclaims a more lucid mind.

Expatriot

It's hot, damned hot, and humid as I make my way down the rocky beach;
the early mornings sea breeze have stopped, keeping comfort out of reach.

The shrimpers are in with their predawn catch and lately the shrimping
hasn't been good;
about half of that of years past,
leaving little for family food.

The gulls are here to greet the boats each screeching "me", "me",
and they bombard the boats with accuracy
just to get some of the catch for free.

At the docks the cats await the fisherman's daily return,
chasing the bravest of the gulls away
hoping that they earn
just a part of the meager load brought to shore today,
if not they'll fake indifference and
simply walk away.

And me, I wait to buy a scoop of shrimp or a blue water fresh fish,
it costs but a few pesos,
not much more than a wish.

When the moonlight begins streaming across the sea's blue-green waves
I will have eaten my evening meal…
and I'll wait for sunlight's promising new day.

Fading (Tom King)

He leans against his faded truck, his cap pulled down and tight,
in faded jeans and faded shirt that look like he slept in them last night.
His cowboy boots have seen better days, heels rounded, the leather worn
and the faded jacket laying on the seat is tattered, well-worn and torn.

A darkly weathered hawkish face with Canyon like wrinkles
and dark blue eyes that could use glasses but when he smiles the eyes crinkle.
His eyes look directly into yours as he speaks,
but his head lowers when he listens,
as if studying and weighing your every word before he gives you his opinion.

A saddle shined by use, a fraid roping strand and leather gloves with holes,
lay in the back of the pickup truck until needed to accomplish his goals.
Grazing a herd of 400, working part-time as well,
from daybreak to dusk in the heat and the cold
struggling against nature's living hell.

His house needs work but his fences are fixed and his windmills all run fine;
Thus, his livelihood is always protected and has been throughout his time.
He pays mostly in cash
from a stash
that is buried somewhere along Miller's branch,
and he ekes out a meager living on his 1,200 acre ranch.

Been married to a half-breed for over 40 years, she works as hard as he,
and it never seems to bother either of them, that brand burned in by society.
A better shot, a better trapper, she does everything she can
to make a better life for her tall, thin and fading ranching man.

Memories fading like his blue jeans, a life worn thin by age,
he fought against the odds of nature never showing any rage;
and as a kid I watch his every move and I'm reminded of just one thing,
there is no one better at what he does, but he's fading fast.....this rancher ol' Tom King.

Garden Wall

The crickets play hide-and-seek on the stone garden wall,
sometimes peering from the stones at the foxtail that grows in the distance;
and here they play until the evening chill of fall,
with both they and the garden offering little resistance.

Fall is sad time for my garden and for the plants and creatures therein,
for summers end signals a time for the new season to harden,
and bring the past season's bounty to an end.

Flowers will shrink and refuse to bloom,
and the playful crickets will disappear,
the vegetable plants will submit to the gloom
as all await the start of a new growing year.

In the warm glow of spring new growth will appear
with summers prizes by nature arranged;
crickets will play among the stones this new year,
forgetting the forthcoming annual seasonal change.

Glass Canyon

Glass canyon, reflecting concrete and steel framing,
your echoes no less than those of nature, but harsher.
No native foliage here, just steel and tin street signs,
signs that tell you when to walk, when to stay still.

Universal light does not play off your walls,
only the incandescent and neon, and those of the
wheeled beasts that traverse your valleys;
the color seldom changing, eventually leading to monochrome.

Yes, the indigenous are here, walking on their Ferragammo's
and covered with synthetic wrappings that indicate their status.
They scale your walls in hydraulic and cabled comfort with a
false pride in reaching predetermined plateaus.

And so glass canyon you will survive, but not for as long
as your natured brethren. The new -indigenous tribe will
wander through your halls, rushing toward their demise
while the ancient ones watch and shake their head.

Haakken

Blue bib overalls and a dirty long-sleeved shirt,
regardless of the temperature, regardless of the work;
he lived along the river among the chest high button weeds,
with bullfrogs, snakes and stinging things, that made their home in the reeds.

A hermit we all called him, because a hermit is what he was;
kept mostly to himself unless working on cash paying short-term jobs.
He ate most of his food from a can, drank vinegar from a tin ladle,
and only the kindness of the town folk kept food upon his table.

This tall and thin old Norwegian, living at the water's edge
in a two room shack, set on blocks, an ungodly place to live.
He's scared all the children, any movement causing them to flee;
he scared some of the grown-ups too, but he never did scare me.

By the end of summer he'd taught me to fish
and why snakes still wiggle when cut in half,
and I taught him how to smile at life, and I taught him how to laugh.
I never found out his story, never learned of his end;
but for one summer growing up along the Sheyenne River,
I had a friend named Haakken!

Harley and Me

1400 miles on my Harley; running to the sun, pushing back at the rain.
High speed 4-lane, slow speed 2-lane, a blur from day to night;
leaving the good land, going to the Badlands.

My arms are numb, my ass number and my ears are tuned to the roar.
My face, calloused by the wind, has a permanent smile as we
challenge the next hill, the next curve.

Gawkers in a green Plymouth, a farmer leaning on his truck;
fourteen head of cattle resting beside me in the shade.
Racing a prairie rattler on this black ribbon, and burying a coyote's
howl with the bike's sound as it cuts the night like a knife blade.

Listening to the music playing in my head and the tempo changes
with each twist of the throttle. Roadside gas, roadside bar, and the
cowboys want to kick my ass…but they don't. Be careful who you
smile at, even if she winks and smiles back!

Heart of a Traveler

I travel because I chose to; it brings excitement to my normally mundane life.
In travel I can be as adventurous as I like, or I can sit peacefully and reflect on
my time; usually there is no one present who can indirectly direct me.

Life is much easier in my travels!

In travel I worry less about life in general; living for this day is the only goal I
have. I've discovered that that which soothes the soul and appeases the gods-
of-random-days is all I need and wish for. My daytime thoughts are of the eve,
my evening thoughts are of the day that follows.

The sea, warm sand and the palm trees are there for only me and represent
a change from the *traffic* of my life; the traffic is what I share with others on
a day-to-day basis. This lazy travel freedom is the selection I chose and it
warms my mind knowing that where I chose is a place that is mine alone.

There is a serene beauty in travel, in the sights and smells, and sounds. And
an unseen comfort which allows me to escape within myself and dream of a
yet unlived adventure, romantic nights, and a happier existence.

The destination is secondary; my mind will wrap-around the location. Soon
my ears will hear the seductive sounds, my eyes will drink-in the sights and
my heart will once again be the heart of a traveler

Iguana

The Bearded Iguana and I stare at each other in a respectful detente. He slowly walks along the stone wall surveying his realm; his multicolored head and crown signaling his place within his mini- kingdom. It's raining on both of us...... it bothers me much more than it bothers him.

We both know he is a magnificent creature! At 2 foot in length, he has a strong upper body which he tends to show off by raising himself on his forefeet, a perfect display of his species and of male arrogance. Even in the damp gray light, his muted colors show their prominence. His body tapers rapidly from the shoulders ending in a point at tales end; a body meant for speed. A female appears behind him and dutifully follows. She's smaller, darker in color, but no less slow. She eyes me cautiously and darts at even the most subtle of my movements, ducking behind the wall every now and then in precaution. He does not! He is wise to the intruding tourist and instinctively sure he can out run, or outwit me, if necessary, for I am in his realm.

And so we play the game. As I move along the opposite wall he moves with me, stopping, when he chooses, simply to display his superiority. Now it's beginning to thunder and the sky is darker with rain clouds, and the wind is increasing. Soon a much more intense rain will begin.......... and it will bother me much more than him!

Island Day

Sun blurred vision, skin with a red tint,
hair dancing the twist with a partner to music
performed by the ocean winds.

Far less clothing than is normally acceptable,
and you notice your feet are truly ugly.
But my companion is beautiful, with a smile
that lights up the day,

Her laugh matches the rhythm of the reggae
playing over the outdoor speakers.
The salty taste of flesh, sweat or salt water (?);
salt water, as confirmed by the scent of her
sea-dampened hair.

Rum punch, the punch apparently named for the phrase
" knock-out punch", goes down way too easy
and you thirst for more.

The shaded side of the palm trees creates a silhouette that
mirrors the shadows the trees cast upon the sand
only minutes earlier…..and a lone pelican makes his last
loud attempt at a meal.

An orange-red sun setting on the water sends a colored,
shimmering trail to my feet.
My beautiful companion and I raise our glasses in a silent
toast to each other….and then a toast to the setting sun to
thank it for the day it delivered.

Island Evening

The waves move the sand in a seemingly random action,
but the tiny grains insist in settling in stylish fashion.
A broken shell floats in resting sunny side up and the
shore birds investigate the possibilities.

Pieces of wood become driftwood, waterlogged then dried by the sun.
A floating coconut glimmers in its green beauty, defiantly contrasting
with the blue Caribbean, and the pelicans make one last voyage before
they rest for the night.

The sun, tired from a hot days work, struggles to set on the sea's horizon,
sending glowing red rays shimmering across the water. It seems as though
the sea resists as it pushes back the sun and cries out for a few more moments
of brightness, of warmth.

A lone fisherman, wading his way back home, walks knee deep,
paralleling the shore and casting a small, weighted net.
Hopefully he will have pockets full of small fish with which
to feed his family by the time the sun rests and the moon awakens.

A mongrel dog trots the beach, scavenging his next free meal;
for him it is a small price to pay for his freedom, and sand crusted,
damp corn chips are a tasty treat on today's hunt. Perhaps, on his
darkened return, an injured sea creature will offer up a more filling repast.

The days wind has quieted now, snuggling in evening's bed with the sun,
and the moon begins to peek out from behind a cloud. It is now the moon's
turn to show the beauty that lies within the darkness that is night,.... and it will
linger until dawn chases it away.

Life in a Bubble

He's wrapped tightly in the arms of society,
where nothing can harm and there are few true needs.
A plastic smile in a plastic world,
where time, hope and life all travel the same speed.

A place of semi-comfort, one where neutral shades control,
leaving little to the imagination, leaving little reason to frown.
A sterile life within a sterile bubble;
just black and white, no vibrant colors around.

A life of the lifeless, mowing a sepia colored lawn
in front of a white house, one just like the neighbors.
A life de jour, like soup de jour,
no spices added for exciting flavors.

But he dreams of islands, of adventurous times;
the life of a diplomat or a spy.
Yes, he dreams that next year he will travel a lot;
but when the time arrives, he won't even try.

He's stuck within the bubble, controlled by the life he chose,
remaining one of the millions of neutrals, the unseen.
And, when the time comes, he will die in that bubble,
regretting that he did not live even one of his dreams.

Lunch with Elvis

A sweltering heat on Beale Street, tourists wiping sweat away
and looking for the closest air conditioned building
to escape humidity's damp grasp.

After a tour of Graceland a king has been de-throned,
assisted by the hanger-on's books. The crown of black
locks is replaced by one of over indulgence; this adds
to middle age changes in voice and body.

Only the early music remains of the man. The ice in my
sweet tea melts too fast and the plastic smile of the waitress
cracks as she calls me "hon" once again. The chicken
salad sandwich in front of me changes to peanut butter and
banana, and when the plastic smile served me I said:
"Thank you....thank you very much".

The tourists continue walking on Beale Street, and still sweating;
each humming the songs of the fifties and sixties as the
Jordanaires sing backup. Then, the black and white image of the
young man who would be king slides into the other side of
my booth....and smiles a sneering smile.

Lynda Bonham
1960

She sits quietly, back to the wall, as you both dine on lime-fish and rice,
drinking warm beer and listening to Perry Como in the island's humid night.

A staccato voice with an accent so pleasing as she whispers her earthly thoughts,
and the softness of the moments spent with her adds to the vacationer's dream.

A disarmingly bright smile framed by dark lips, high cheekbones that disappear
into dark hair.

Sliding, graceful movements as she walks towards me, grasps my hand in hers,
and raises me to my feet.

Dark eyes moist with passion as the day ends, leaving the balance of the evening to
anticipation.

Her soft dark skin has the aroma of coconut oil, and she wraps her long arms
and legs around me.

This dream will be repeated for six more days and love and laughter will fill the
nighttime hours as the music of the island fills my mind

.... and as she fills my senses.

Memories

Memories are not enough, they fade over time,
and the content changes and rearranges
as they are played back in your mind.

Sights and sounds once held dear are blurred by time's
passing role, and that which is left is mixed and matched
within the confines of the soul.

Yes, I have the memories when times are good,
memories when times are rough, memories are all that I have,
but memories are not enough.

Memories

Memories from the past,
scenes and times that stand alone,
within the heart and soul they are meant to last,
for in the heart and soul they've found a home.

Faces filled with tears and laughter,
warm breezes, thunderous storms,
each replayed in the mind forever after ,
and each recalled in original form.

Some bring comfort, others pain,
each memory reshapes the soul
by making it stronger so do not disdain,
for the memories are there to make one whole.

Memory Awakening

Movement within the shadows of my mind, a memory awakening,
asserting its place and demanding attention at this time,
the stream of its content is mine for the taking.

Did I summon it forth, or did it arrive on its own,
is there a need I subconsciously want to fulfill?
Should I allow it to stay, should I condone,
or do I stave off this latest mind- chill?

The decision is mine, my priorities are set,
"no interference should cloud my mind".
But the memory insists that its conditions be met,
as well as demands more than equal time.

Having no choice, I reluctantly give in
and let the memory have its way.
To see me now as I am, or what I have been,
as memory turns night into day.

Metamorphic

I am evolving, ever so slowly, into a new person.
The gradual changes come with age and events;
most free me from my self-imposed prison
and viewing the subtleties is time well spent.

I think I understand why, but not how,
this metamorphosis is taking place;
not sure if the growth is right for now
but sure that it will be in some future space.

My archaic thoughts are changing, like age upon my face,
shifting premises, ideals, and with hopes rearranging ,
falling perhaps from a bygone era's grace.

Promises new, or simply forgetting the past,
fear and excitement as a new beginning unfolds;
the life and times that once were cannot last
as I seek to renew my spirit and soul.

Metaphors

Poetry is comprised of metaphors, some unintentional,
describing love and life in terms less real,
leaving true words of reality back as unmentionable,
and flowing into a mindscape of life seen surreal.

The metaphors are many between the spiritual and the physical,
shedding little light regarding direct truth.
Obscure phrases not unlike faces in a dream's recall,
and hidden within is the object honesty of our youth.

And therein lies the poet's changes, for he steers the poetic helm,
turning words and phrases, life and love rearranges
into the metaphors that do abound.

Mexico, 1960

I can't speak her language but I can read her body;
She can't speak my language, but reads my eyes.
Two, too young to enter the cantina, choose the warm moonlight.
Without speaking we walk the few short blocks to the beach, as
the ever-present dogs announce each milestone of our journey.

Clouds create a pattern with the moonlight as the waves lap at the shore, and
the old fishing boats make moaning sounds as they rock to the music of the sea.
For some unknown reason, the combination of sounds create a symphony as the
walk carries us deeper into the mood we've set.

We are both hungry, hungry for the pleasures that love brings; we touch
hands and continue with our walk with hearts that beat rapidly with anticipation.
Within a mile, the few lights of the village grow increasingly dim then fade to a
single light. Only then do we face each other and hesitantly kiss.

The kiss is exciting, passionate, but not as exciting as her arms wrapped around
my sunburned naked torso,
for there is both heat and cooling within her touch.

The kiss seems to last forever, but yet not long enough. Our lips separate for a
brief moment then hurriedly return to the sensuous passion of the moonlight.

Soon our breathing is more intense and breath's sounds are co-mingled, and,
regardless of whose breath you hear, the breathing is one of restless pleasure.
Soon a flurry of hands move along the landscape of our bodies; again not sure
of whom is touching what, but as though we are of one body.

We clumsily struggle to beachside grass and collapse into a night of saltwater
symphonies. Never speaking a verbal language, we communicate with hearts
and souls, with sighs and guttural sounds that are universal in nature. And in
the early dawn we retrace our steps back to the village, and silently promise
each other yet another concert by the sea.

Modern Madness

Throwing paint on a canvas,
words splattered on paper;
all from the mind of passion,
all from a mind of modern madness.

Breaking glasses in the fireplace,
high-speed midnight rides in a black convertible,
blowing kisses at the moon.

Three chord rock and roll on a cheap guitar;
a skydiving, race car driving, zip-line tour
of life. A barroom brawl while reading Shakespeare,
a pirouette on a motorcycle, a hunger
never, ever, satisfied.

A life that is too short, then too long.
A life too loud, then too quiet;
constantly too confusing in the
searing heat of *now*.

Mollie Toothless, Part 11

In visiting this place and looking down on the arid floor below, the temperature is seasonally cooling there, while on the upper rim there will soon be snow.

Mollie sits out in front of her Hogan, eye squinting from afternoon light, and she speaks softly of her history, her land, and if left to, would talk long into the night.

Mollie lives in a distant Canyon, miles from a good road or hope; her entire life spent on the reservation, living up high on the canyon's north slope.

A childless marriage to a good man, the two worked a lifetime side-by-side, just to eke out a meager existence, until 10 years ago when the good man died.

Now Mollie spends most of her time alone save for sporadic visits from the tribe; most of whom never made it to the old man's funeral, due to the great distance up the canyon's side.

Her soft voice can sometimes speak the words of her nearly lost native tongue, her husband was a wind talker when the big war was won; but some of the words get lost in her mind and in struggling to speak with an ancient voice, she gives up over time.

Mollie sits by her Hogan counting her sheep, and counting the days until the spirit will come, to help her find the way to visit those friends who passed on; to visit those ghosts with their smiling faces and kind words, those who greet her with each new dawn.

In her sad heart she prays each day that today will be the best day to go, for within the warmth of the place the spirit will lead her, she knows her soul will glow.

Yes, it's getting colder now in the arid had land below, and soon Mollie's Hogan will be covered, in a dusting of white winter snow. They will find her then starring up at the sky with a slight smile upon her face; for now the Spirit is walking beside her, taking her to a happier place.

Mother's Day (and night)

She stares into the morning mirror looking for a reflection of her perfect life;
to the outside world she is a wonder woman, a mother and a perfect wife.
But within the confines of reality her self-appointed failures dominate her will,
and she reaches into the cabinet for a handful of reflection altering pills.

The house is not perfect enough, her late teens children have gone separate ways,
and her husband's only affection is shown in the light of in- the- public day.
The coldness of her empty life leaves her with a chill,
and she reaches for the cabinet with its wonderful warming pills.

A life on the brink, evenings spent alone, lying to herself
and to her friends on the telephone. Yes, everything is fine, (she
takes another sip from the glass), isn't life supposed to be this way…but still (?),
then another trip to the cabinet to reflect on those happiness pills.

Things will change tomorrow, but tomorrow never comes,
and she moves through each day and into the future, with a mind forever numb.
The days are long and the nights are longer as she reflects on life's valleys and hills,
the struggle would be much more difficult without her cabinet full of pills.

So she swears to stop the abuse and turn her life around,
to live up to her perception of the reflections to be found;
but she never tries, never fights back, and probably never will,
for down the hall in the cabinet, is a supply of life changing pills.

Mustang

He stands with his nose to the wind, nostrils flared, and pawing the ground. He senses me, but as yet hasn't seen me hidden in a small stand of soft pines; still he knows I'm near. The mares feel his tension and are skittish, their heads up and turning hoping to help him spot the hidden danger.

I watch him and he knows it. We are a lot alike that Mustang and me. We love our freedom, hate the feeling of being trapped, and live for the sunrise. And nature has made us both guarded and suspicious.

I think he spotted me, he's glaring and shivers are moving down his flanks! And in a second he'll be off with his mares close behind. Me, I'll just wait until the next time; this is just a game between me and that old Mustang.

He and I have been playing this game for maybe two years. Who knows how many years, or how many people, have played this game with him before I came along. He is much more seasoned at this than I am, and most of the time he outwits me. But in these two years I learned a few of his habits, the places he and his harem like to visit.

I look for him every time I'm out. In the fall he and the mares are easier to find; sometimes, if I'm lucky, I can follow a trail of steaming scat. And I work hard at staying in the background and downwind. He works hard at standing on the highest point, head high, and nose to the wind. Although my Lakota friends say they've seen it, I've never seen him in a box canyon, he's far too wise for that!

So we continue to play the game, a game with no winners, no losers. And we continue to learn much about each other. In the quiet of the night as I close my eyes to sleep, I see that old Mustang and I wonder, when he closes his eyes does he see me too?

Mustang, II

His head held high he gallops away leading me on a dusty chase, the mares just
slightly ahead of him run faster as they try to leave me in this place.
The sound of the thundering hooves grow dim as I rein- back and watch him run,
and he and his harem kicking up dust as they gallop into the sun.

Down into the valley then up on the hillside where he slows his pace to look back,
he watches there from the distance then turns, and gets the mares back on track.
A much easier gait as he reaches the top, for the distance is on his side,
and there he waits and watches, as I continue my much slower ride.

He senses his speed and spirit will keep me just far enough behind
as he moves the mares ahead of him and drives them up the next incline.
The wind in his face lets him know I am here and he wrinkles his nose at my scent;
but there is far enough space between us now, and the mares can rest for they're
physically spent.

We stare at each other from opposite sides and a smile crosses my face, I raise hat in
hand in salute of his cunning and prepare for another day's race.
We've been doing this for some time him and I, playing Fox and hound, and nobody
wins;
and I pray he keeps running with his mares forever, and none of us ever catches him.

Nearly Forty Years Ago

She was striking in appearance, dark and tall, with big eyes and sensuous lips,
she of perfect posture, she with the swaying hips and perfect smile.
Her accent was a mixture of Island Black, with just a hint of French,
and a laugh that gave my spirit a lift, a lift that lasted for quite a while.

She sang in a band, although her voice wasn't particularly good;
I think she was on stage strictly for her looks.
But late at night in the smoky bar her lyrics set the mood
that made me question my decision to live my life by the books.

Her long and sinuous body moved in rhythm to the music,
and her bedroom voice sang a whispery song
that conjured images of two life's lost; of love
happiness and hope, now gone.

So I sat and listened in the island rain, to the voice
that somehow matched her body and this particular time.
The music and the lyrics fit the night like a velvet glove,
and she has fit comfortably, for nearly forty years, in my mind.

That dark lady of song, the one with the sultry voice, became my
friend, and over time she married a island man.
Our life's grew-up together, although miles and miles apart
and just before she died she called me to make up for time's demands
and she told me that nearly forty years ago,
I unknowingly had captured her heart.

I spoke with her daughter not long ago; she found a few of my poems
in her mother's belongings;
along with my name and telephone number, plus a few other things.
But what surprised me the most was her daughter's point of view,
for in our conversation she said,
"My mother's one great love in life…..was you"!

Next Victim

The Spirit of War awakens with a nasty growl,
and searches for the next victim.
Countries are devoured from within and without,
friends turned into enemies, and foolish pride prevails.

Homicide and genocide are tolerated by those on the "right" side;
logic is destroyed, compassion is crushed,
and the innocent on both sides suffer equally.

With this rabid dog unleashed, one land will be laid bare
while another celebrates.
But, as history foretells, the celebration may be short lived;
for when this evil spirit is once again wakened,
he may well chose them as the next victim.

Nyx

Nyx, goddess of the night, daughter of Chaos, interrupting the sun
with darkness shutting out the light .
Nyx, causing me to try and sleep, but restful sleep never comes;
her movements in the dark cause my soul to weep in the night.

She forces me to become an Oneiroi, one of the Tribe of Dreams,
by using her father's random methods to create a sweating body,
a fitful sleep,… a silent scream.

Nyx, causing the darkest of the dark, driving the night to last even longer;
there are no rules here floating on night's ark,
only the ghostly faces of the spirits that wander.

She controls the tempo and the time as I flow through the dark on a river of black,
with erratic scenes playing through my mind
until daylight demands equality, then I can take my mind back.

Nyx, although you are Chaos' daughter, I will win you over in time;
then out of Chaos will come order,
and with order, peace in my mind.

Warren K. Olson

Of Moss Covered Walls (and Life)

Over the years moss has collected on the old stone wall
giving the spiders and crickets a place to live,
changing the stones colors like tapestry in a castle hall,
the moss altering the space with all that it gives.

The muted green against the browns and grays
brings natural beauty to the site,
and as nature wishes, the colors change day- to- day
controlled by the manipulations of the sun's light.

In the evening the moss changes patterns
as the moonlight dances through the trees,
like ink spilled on white paper and splattered
the night configuration is un-confining and free.

And so color and shape are altered by nature's changes,
a blending that sets *fixed* things free;
a structured event that time re-arranges
and perhaps that's the way life's meant to be.

Patterns that appear to be set may be tossed
and color can change with the light;
like structures of stone are softened by moss
changes, some subtle, may re-shape our life.

Peter Tall Oak

Peter Tall Oak was a throwback
to the time when his people roamed free.
But he lived in this age among the pines in the outback,
after fighting in the Asian jungle for you and me.

Peter got cancer in his 50s; nothing to do
but wait for the Great Spirit to call him home.
Still he gave what he could to the tribe, his people,
and lamented "no freedom to roam".

He talked to the priest at the mission,
"no funeral for me", he said;
"let me be mourned like my ancestors,
laid on a poplar pyre with three feathers placed by my head".

But the white men wouldn't allow it
and their laws now governed his land;
it didn't matter what Peter and his soul did covet,
didn't matter that he was a veteran.

He died on Tuesday in October, still fighting for his own rights.
None of us reported his death to the coroner,
we let him lay peacefully thru' the night.
The next morning we built a poplar platform and
carried Peter to a remote Butte near the water;
singing and chanting we released his spirit and three feathers
to roam free in the hereafter.

Prairie Night

In the cool quiet of this prairie night all is still;
The only noise is the rustling of native grasses, made to dance
by the movement music of an evening breeze.
All surrounding shapes are cloaked in silhouette threads,
leaving them one color against the horizon.

The half-moon peeks from behind the only cloud in the sky,
lighting the way for the human mind to travel, travel
the true depth of this place. For here in the night, distance is
measured in a time sequence, and not in feet or miles.

The prairie grass has an evening dampness to it
and the night's perfume an earthen smell.
The moonlight offers only selective light reflecting off of
the lighter colored natural objects that abound.......
And the cool quiet will stay until the dawn.

Puerto Morales

The palm trees movements are ever so graceful, a gentle swaying that
mesmorizes
the eye and mind.
The sea, calm now, has only white-edge curls caressing the sands, and the
moonlight
touches all that it meets.

Looking close into the water at the waters edge, a school of jellyfish floats
like deflated opaque balloons as they roll in and out in synchronous fashion.
The jellyfish, and an occasional sea urchin, replace the tourists and expatriates
at this time of night.

Farther down the beach an errant coconut rides the surf in several times
before it's planted in the sand. There, if it were not for humankind's
interference, it could make the beach its home and cool the sand crabs
in future times.

The gulls, pelicans and shorebirds are still, resting safely after the frigate
birds last patrol of the evening.
The only sound is that of the waves whispering to the shore before
their brief, damp dalliance.

Yes, things are quietly normal here in the late night air.
Nature's activities, save for that of the ocean, have come to rest.
In a few short hours daylight will arrive, alarm those in repose,
and natures sequence will start anew.

Rain in Paradise

The rain rolls across the sea, the sea doesn't mind, but the tourists do.
The gardens of this man-made Eden welcome the droplets,
    and the tourist's complain.

People, still dripping from their swim, dash madly to the nearest open palapa
and take shelter; do they think the rain will drown them
    quicker than the sea?

Here, in this hand formed paradise, the one-week, or once-in-a-lifetime, visitor
detests nature that is natural; they prefer the molded, the sculpted,
    and perhaps the plastic they have back home.

For me, the mini- storm is amazing! A small break in the clouds,
and the sun makes the waves shine like diamonds as they kiss the shore.
And from the east, the dark clouds, wind and rain change the seas colors,
    creating a moving kaleidoscope of blues, greens, and frothy white.

When the rain reaches the beach, the white sand beneath my feet is darkened by
the dampness and miniature pockmarks are imprinted by the raindrops
    creating an ever changing landscape.

The tourists have left the beach, to the bars, to their rooms to watch CNN,
and I'm left alone with the scavenger birds, alone with the sea, the wind, and
    the rain... and it's wonderful!

Red Butte

Windswept red plateau, with your scared sides rising high
above the valley's floor.
Erosion crevices that change hues as mother earth revolves,
each revolution creating a kaleidoscope in eye and mind.

History is hidden within your colors, history sometimes reveled
by exposure to the wind or the rapid descent of infrequent cloudbursts.
A history begrudgingly surrendered.

Barren, save for your Pines that are worn like a crown,
and silent, save for the wind.
You stand majestically alone, a ceremonial alter cast by nature,
not man.

You have ruled this valley since the beginning of time
… and you will stand until time ceases!

Red Corvette

On the road, heading back home, in a *country* frame of mind;
stopped for gas in a nameless town and decided to rest there for the night.
After a heartburn dinner, a country bar, stepping back in time where a
white t-shirt, dusty jeans and well worn boots look right.

Music blaring from a jukebox, men outnumber the women five to one,
and country songs about lost love, just aching to be sung.
Music for dancing, music for singing, music taking me back in time
to better nights in better places, when everything was fine.

The bar maid has long dark hair and smiled with a slight overbite,
big dark eyes, a raspy voice and jeans that fit a bit too tight;
Stuck here in this nameless town about 50 miles from nowhere,
she only has her past, no future, and she's the only one who cares.

Except for me, a stranger in a red Corvette, with his dusty boots in the trunk;
by midnight we're singing country songs and both of us are a little drunk.
I tell her to leave this nowhere town, there's a whole world out there to get,
and the bar maid wants travel that world with me in a red Corvette.

Early in the daylight I have to move on, like to travel on my own time;
I tell I'll be back some day, if not in person, then in a country frame of mind.
I know we had a damn good time, neither feeling much regret,
But I'm willing bet it wasn't me she loved, I'm sure it was the red Corvette.

Reverend Connor

The Reverend Connor was a pious man,
fire and brimstone is what he preached
while waiting for God to send a message to him,
for the Lord's true intent was beyond his reach.

On Sundays he would damn the congregation
with his loud voice scaring the children,
pleading with each member to beg for salvation
before God brought this shameless world to an end.

The Reverend Connor led an alternate life
with his clerical robes tucked safely away.
A two year affair with another man's wife,
using God's words to help lead her astray.

Connor received his just reward
in the vein of a non-biblical passage;
shot by the husband of an unfaithful wife,
Connor finally received God's message!

Rhythm of the Rails

The railroad car sways gently, rocking your body from the waist up
and you perform a sitting hula.

It doesn't matter if you're tired or not, within minutes the movement
makes you close your eyes, if for no other reason than to concentrate
on the movement and the rhythm.

The clickity-clack of the steel wheels rolling over the track joints
creates a beat that is transferred to your feet.

The railcar is facing backwards and a glance tells you where you've been,
but doesn't allow you the pleasure of seeing what lays ahead. It's like waving
a perpetual goodbye.

The movements and sounds play in your mind like an ancient tribal dance;
then you drift-off to the mesmerizing rhythm of the rails.

Santiago

Santiago is a shaman, he keeps the spirits balanced
through the toss of a few bones.
With some lines drawn on the earth the spirit world is challenged,
and he can read your life with his magic stones.

He is ever so careful to read, then react with the proper chant
and burning grasses adding to the cure,
providing the spirits chose to grant
that which will leave your soul pure.

Every move is calculated, every bone and stone must find the right place;
a medicine bag full of history articulated
by the magic that abounds in the shaman's space.

He's old, this shaman, with few who will follow in his path,
for there is no money or glory to be found, and only time
will determine if the magic lasts,
and only time will prove the healing profound.

You believe the old man for you see history through his eyes
and inside you know his power is true, as he chants
over bones under smoky night skies
and prays the right spirit comes to you.

Shadow within Shadow

There are moments in my life with double shadows, darker within dark;

wherein the history of my soul is written in contrasting shades of gray,

telling long held tales directly from the heart, and to my own mind simply displayed..

The double walled shadows create an illusion, in case someone else happens in.

Their movement is mixed, adding to the confusion of what I am, or have been.

Still, there is a certain comfort in the dark shadows, for theirs is a movement of force.

For as long as I'm able I'll deal with that darkness, for it's become part of my life's natural course.

Shining Season

This is the *Shining Season*, when hearts are light
and family and friends are held dearer;
this is a time of hope and compassion
as we draw universal love ever nearer.
This is the time to reaffirm our faith,
in God, in nature, in man
as we re-tell the story of a child born in a manger
in the small town of Bethlehem.
Now are the moments to celebrate
and to pray for mankind in a future tense,
for faith, love, hope and compassion are not so much taught
as they are learned through experience.
My wish is for *all* to hold tight to this light,
to treasure these moments so dear,
and to share the light with everyone you meet
throughout the coming year.
Make every season a Shining Season,
use your heart to mend every fence;
for faith, love, hope and compassion are not so much taught,
… as they are learned through experience.

Silent Scream

Did you ever *hear* a silent scream?
It arrives in the dark of night;
its position lurking within the content of a dream,
not leaving until the mind declares daylight.

Did you ever *see* a silent scream,
its face contorted in pain;
where one may watch the face change shape,
like wax melting under a candle's flame.

Did you ever *experience* a silent scream?
it gives the body a chill;
and agony takes place within the brain
making the experience a living hell!

Spring in Dogdom

Even my dogs know when spring arrives. It may be due to the chirping of the birds in the backyard, or the delectable dead bird treats they find under or behind the hedge. Even in the dampness of spring showers, the dogs move with a lighter, happier step. I think they tire of winter as much as I do; winter seems heavy, long, and boring to our household.

The dogs also like when I rake fall's and winter's deposits. They run through the yard redistributing windrows of leaves and small branches I so carefully craft; they always manage to find a long forgotten toy among these lines of spring. A miniature stuffed "squeaky" toy, damp and faded, becomes a homecoming celebration as they swoop it up and give it a tour of their mini- kingdom. Realizing that the rake is the catalyst for re-found friends and treats, they follow me to be the first to welcome any new and interesting finds; my dogs function as the archaeologists of the animal kingdom.

When we break for lunch, we all need a slight cleaning; me by removing old sneakers and brushing pant legs, and they by having muddied paws wiped and the odd mixture of spring yard waste and residue brushed from their under underbellies. With each quick brush they investigate the mother lode of particles released from their magnetic fur and end up tracking it in the house anyway.

After lunch we all spring into action much sooner than during the days of winter. They feel the need to explore their newly reclaimed space, to pick up and trace odors that have been released by the *magic* rake. And, while I fret over a yard worn thin by their antics, they race through the windrows on the scent of the squirrel that will antagonize them from today until winter's grip.

At the end of today's busy schedule, they lie on the top deck in the late afternoon sun and survey their realm. Both dogs emit a lazy sigh and wait for a new day of spring adventure.

Warren K. Olson

St. Kitts, 1976

It's too loud now as the revelers have joined the chorus of the parade;
too loud and too hot! Everyone is sweating, even us, the smart ones
standing on the shady side of the street.

The bar remains open, but most of the staff has migrated outside,
drawn by the music and other sounds. The beat is contagious, as is
the mood. There are brightly colored costumes, with strings of
beads that shine like the sweat on black bodies; the bodies dance
to honor a Saint that their ancestors never knew.

There is music everywhere, in the streets, in the bar, and on the
lips of my fellow watchers, and it mingles into a cacophony of
conflicting sounds.

The street vendors have stopped hawking their wares and sing along
while gawking at the ladies in the parade; the vendor's bodies moving
to the music, their minds mesmerized by both sight and sound.

Even the lazy street dogs are up and wandering through the crowd,
capturing a fallen morsel now and then. So far it has been a good
day for them.

The music, the colorful sights and smells continue in the humidity
and one is drawn into the kaleidoscope of the afternoon. By now
my beer is warm and I have a hunger for street food. But I wait
and watch; I'd hate to miss the next entry, it may just be the best,
and I wouldn't want to miss that!

And so I watch, and wonder if there is a magic to this day.
Is it me, the beer, the island and its people, or the carnival
that has my mind dancing?
The answer is simply, "Yes!"

Starved Rock Morning

A sharp, cold wind pushes its way into the Canyon causing the foliage to dance. The steep walls allow but a sliver of sunlight to touch the earthen floor. The air is damp and the trail wet; leaves bow under the soggy air, and the birds are silent.

Half way up to the rim, the air begins to warm as the sun fills a wider swath, and you notice insects moving within the ground cover. Nearing the top, one hears the songs of flight, and squirrels scamper to the safety of the closest tree.

Reaching the top, the trail stands before you then disappears with its sharp turns and sharp changes in elevation. Wind-scarred boulders line the trail, their positioning a gift from nature. To the right and left, tall trees with their less fortunate, fallen brethren resting on meadow grass; the fallen, with dried trunks and limbs, serve as incubators for an extensive family of wild mushrooms.

Along the rim, rays of sunlight penetrate the canopy, warming the trail and the body. High overhead an Eagle soars, surveying his realm, while below the Illinois River flows slowly toward its ultimate destination.

The air retains its crispness, as does the frightened movements of a startled white tailed doe. You and the doe are surprised at the presence of the "other". Soon the trail will lead you downward into another Canyon, to another treasure, where even the faintest of voice echoes within nature's walls.

One can become mentally lost here, and let history rule the mind; from geological formations to the indigenous, and to today's tourists, 10,000 years stand before you. Time for a hand warming cup of coffee as you contemplate the rest of this adventure, for this beauty goes on for miles!

The Legend's Song

The Legends sing songs of the prairie,
telling a history older than mankind,
of tall prairie grass and transparent streams
created in earlier ancient times.

They tell of past winters and summers,
of shaggy beasts that roamed in vast herds,
and of the people of the Seven Nations
who first walked over the prairie earth.

They sing about a people betrayed,
of lies and a dishonorable fate
from a group they called white eyes,
and the Seven Nations collapsed under the white eyes' weight.

The Legends tell of the lost spirits of their people,
doomed to wander a new manicured prairie, nothing like the past,
searching for a body the spirits can call a home,
and praying that somehow the Seven Nations will last.

Twilight

In twilight there is certain calm,
a hectic day has been put aside
and it is too early to consider the dark of the night.

Here in the soft glow of transition one can
reflect on the past and plan for the future.
Although the daylight has dimmed, twilight offers
its own beam of wisdom, and sharper intuitive knowledge.

In twilight I can sit with my dogs and the three
of us emit a collective sigh. The dogs survey their realm
and I rest my eyes and *see* with my mind.

Twilight is a quiet, happy time for me and signals a break
at day's end, no instant stop. Twilight is a time to slow down;
like putting the paddle in the canoe and drifting with the current.
In twilight I can look back and see the day as ripples in this silent moment.

Loss

A Desert Storm

Sitting quietly on the deck I watch a rare summer storm approach then the rapid rain descends coating red rocks and bringing new growth.

The birds take shelter within the resort's trees, seeking damp refuge from the storm, and when the deluge so swiftly passes they sing at their melodic norm.

Recently my life has been changed by that I can't control, I saw my own storm coming and its dampness has covered my soul.

Perhaps like the birds and the desert I can find something positive within the storm, and with the resulting rainfall my sad soul will be re-born.

Will I find inner peace, will my mind-storm wash away the grime, like the birds and the desert floor I'm sure I will overtime.

But for now like the cactus I'll wait, let my life follow its natural form; be patient my mind and pray that you find new growth after the desert storm.

Babylon

Once I led the perfect life in the gardens of Babylon
where I strolled among the flowers and saw the dew at dawn;
where towering tiers of beauty grew on happiness alone,
then the darkening skies of a desert storm entered my Babylon.

The desert sands blew steadily until the pathways disappeared.
The hot breath of the desert wind wilted flowers far and near,
which caused the magnificent palms to appear to stand alone.
Where once there was beauty now only shadows visited Babylon.

One could only watch as the beauty ebbed away,
felled by the sands of a strong desert storm that passed along it's way.
Now paradise is lost and the beauty turned to rugged stone
and the space that is left, in the hollow of the earth,
was once the gardens of Babylon.

Can the gardens come back, will they return, before I pass away,
or will the pillars of sand-scared rocks be nature's new display?
Look, near the top of the largest rock rises a flower all alone,
perhaps it's the start of what will be the heart of the *new* gardens of Babylon.

Depression

It comes over me as a shadow, like a cloud blocking the sun's light
changing my mental shape and perspectives, changing day into night.

Lethargy covers my little world like a cloak draped over normal life,
remaining for what seems like forever, offering but brief glimpses of hope's
light.

Inactivity rules this time, and that is truly just not me,
for I am normally active, within the scope of normalcy

This lasts until it runs its course, no "trigger" in or out,
displacing parts of me with questions and unusually full of doubt.

I've learned to live with in these times, to get by on my own,
but a stronger fear in envelops my mind; what if this becomes my comfort
zone?

Still, I am one of the lucky ones, for although I feel the cold wind of sorrow,
I hold tight to this repetitive sequence with its promise of a better tomorrow.

And so depression and melancholy may visit me, as unwelcome as they are,
for I see sunlight in the distance, its light no brighter than a star.

The path is steep, the headwinds strong, as I make my way,
but I move forward step by step, toward a lifetime's better day!

Dining Alone in Paradise

They sit smiling at each other from across the candlelight,
three couples spaced throughout the dining room;
two holding tight to the magic of the night
as I watch enviously… and dine alone.

A young couple, married or not, with lust or love in their eyes
drink a toast to this, their time and place
and turn to view the starlit night sky,
while I dine alone… remembering a fading smiling face.

The middle-aged couple are not in sync,
perhaps time has made their life a folly;
she smiles and nods a lot as he has too much to drink,
as I dine in the company of a glass of wine… and my melancholy.

The older couple have all that most of us want,
an attentive and loving mate,
and like most starcrossed lovers everywhere they feel the urge to flaunt,
as I sit and stare at an empty chair… and silently curse my fate.

This is not easy, dining alone under tropical skies by the sea.
But I have to get used to being on my own for this is what the gods have handed me.
But I won't forget happier times when laughter filled the table,
and I promise to remember dining together… for as long as my mind is able.

And although there may be sadness within this night
I have survived dining alone at paradise's table!

I Should Have Said I Love You
(One More Time)

I should have said "I love you" one more time;

told you how glad I was that you were mine.
I could have given more and taken less,
although you didn't seem to mind;
I should have said, "I love you," one more time!

Its so easy to let the little things slip away
as we move through the moments of each day,
to forget what's truly important
until one day you find
I should have said, "I love you," one more time!

Now you're gone, it's too late to get love back
and I sit in the darkness of the blind,
remembering the good times
and all we left behind,
and I should have said, "I love you," one more time!

Internal Conflict

The battle within me rages on,
a conflict between heart and mind;
brewing what may be the perfect storm,
for the clouds have been building for some time.

Anger, self-directed, over my perception of *me*.
Was it weakness or simply wanting out,
to clear my mind, to set it free
that led me to this place and filled with doubt ?

A dark decision had to be made, and I chose!
Did I take a life or set a soul free;
therein, the proverbial fork in the road,
and in my mind, I chose wisely.

But in my heart I'm not certain,
was it my right to direct this "end"?
Now and forever I shall carry this burden,
a strong mind, but a heart that may never mend!

A continuous search for enlightenment,
for an answer that never comes.
Was I wrong, was I right, was it providence (?)
… and the battle rages on!

Jericho

Walls, fashioned by me, for me;
defensive in nature and protecting me
from outside interference and
keeping most of my emotions in.
Walls that keep outsiders out,
their only access is granted with my permission.
Even when access is allowed
the selected few enter a courtyard,
there to be confronted by yet another set of walls.

The walls have done their job over the years,
allowing me the privilege
of selecting just whom to let pass,
and what emotions to let out;
the walls are all about control!

The events of the past few years
have drastically altered my fortress.
Those events have left several cracks,
promoting deterioration and, in some cases,
causing wall segments to crumble.
For in my search self enlightenment,
I have allowed too many in,
and too much closely- guarded information out.
Each of these movements accelerate
the eventual demise of my wall system.

My self-imposed Jericho may well come tumbling down,
leaving me exposed to the elements.
I'm not sure I like this, but I have no choice,
it must be done to find the real *me*!
Another battle rages on and Joshua is at the gate.
Perhaps it is time to let Joshua claim the spoils of victory!

77

Lifestorm

The warning sounds of a distant thunder,
lightening crossing the sky;
the wind grows stronger and colder
as a storm approaches your life.

The winds of change come blowing in
wreaking havoc in your life plans,
leaving pockmarks on the future
like raindrops on the sand.

Take heed my friend, take warning
of what the distant thunder brings.
For the winds of force direct the course
of your very being.

Plans made will become plans lost,
and your life will be reformed
by the energy and movement
of a passing lifetime storm.

Lost Love

Darker walls within darkened halls,
the damp aroma of musty air;
silent voices, silent bells each giving a silent call
and no one listens because no one cares.

Mistakes were the cause in creating this gloom,
turning brightness into a mind-numbing gray,
and demons dance to the undertaker's tune
as the night over-shadows day.

The dark sea swells under constant rain,
storm clouds obscure the sun.
What is left is *lost love* pain,
and the first day has just begun!

Midnight in the Darkened Cathedral

Midnight in a darkened Cathedral,
a ghostly choir sings chants in the night;
each chant recants the mystery…
of two recently shattered lives.

When did the forces of evil and sadness determine
a need for change in the norm,
allowing two lives to be abruptly altered
by the heart- rendering violence…
of a midnight storm.

Voices clashing in the darkness, a choir directed from hell.
Eerie sounds in the darkened Cathedral…
as fate rings the midnight bell.

Cold winds pass through stained-glass windows;
the moon is captured by clouds;
the choir grows increasingly louder….
as you scream, "Death be not proud"!

"For one who was loved has been taken"; and
the scenes and night sounds are surreal,
as the choir sings loud in the echoing emptiness…
at midnight in the darkened Cathedral.

Only One?

The staff is polite but amazed that I am here among the lovers, in a tropical paradise, alone. At every meal there is the same polite question, "*Only one?*" It is as though they've never witnessed this before; it is an anomaly to most, and apparently a phenomenon to some. I know this can't be true, but it is the way the question makes me feel.

Why would this man travel alone to their "all-inclusive" paradise? Does he not see the breakfast tables are full of two or more? At dinner he stares through his glass of wine and the romantic candlelight into the dark Caribbean. They are cautious about intruding; in fact, they would rather intrude upon the lovers than on the man dining alone. I smile a friendly smile to assure them that all is well; they return a more sympathetic smile, but their eyes question. Yes, tour guides, bartenders, taxi drivers, and shopkeepers all express the same questioning eyes. Only a language barrier keeps them from asking and me from explaining, why there is *only one*.

Perhaps this is why I prefer the jungle; there is no one there to ask the question, "*Only one*"? The iguanas and the crocodiles don't care, the birds continued to sing, and the plant life doesn't change because there is *only one*. In fact, the jungle and the ruins seem to appreciate *only one*, for one is not that much of an intrusion. Even in the off-the-beaten-path villages, one tourist is welcome; more than one makes the people uncomfortable.

One is not bad when you grow to accept it; the problem rests with convincing others!

Orchestrated Grief

There is within me a molten anger, anger over past events, and this symphony I am playing was written without my input; I function only as a percussionist. Had I been allowed to arrange this piece the music would have been more dramatic, with no soft and melodic reprises, and with a sharp, crashing, ending crescendo! This orchestra has too many wind instruments and they don't play loud enough. My rendition would have more brass, deep and stirring drums, and a more thunderous body.

But then, I am not the composer. I am a mere pickup player, just filling a chair. The elaborate orchestration is not so much for the music as it is for altering my perception, to make me play within the confines of the piece placed before me.

There is no clear path between my, and the phantom composer's, interpretation of grief. His is one of soft classical expression while mine is more in Beethoven's realm. The music of my grief has depth, depression, and explosiveness to it; my grief is one of anger and pain!

Still, I continue to play, to chime in as directed, for the conductor demands my presence. But within the darkness of my mind I compose a piece more suitable to what I'm feeling... and I will play it in my own time!

Pedestal

I placed her there upon her death;
high above, beyond reach and out of touch.
No fault would I find, nor would I let you!

Now I realize she was human
and with the warts we all carry.
This doesn't mean I loved her less... or more,
I just humanized that love.

The aura, the protective light shinning on her
has cracked, its opening is obvious.
In time I will offer my hands in assistance,
helping her down from the pedestal
and into memory's reality,
for that is where we both need to be!

Survivor

Within the death comes darkness to the survivor, a chill upon the soul, a fog in the mindscape, disoriented to distraction, a world turned upside down;

too many decisions to be made and too little time to make them.

Now there is one less, and the duet has turned to a solo. The departed rests peacefully; the survivor suffers from an anxious heart, and anxious mind, and the anxiety manifests into sleeplessness.

A constant wave of melancholy persists, broken temporarily by kind and thoughtful words spoken by family and friends. And toughest of all is when you are alone with your thoughts.

Memories blast through your mind like flashbulbs going off and you struggle to hold tight to the good ones. You force the bad thoughts out..... but they don't really leave, they pop up and try to smother the good.

The days drag and the nights seem endless. Time somehow becomes an enemy.

Daily chores are really chores now, almost painful; there are too many of them and most seem difficult at best. The bad thoughts still linger but have lost some of their strength.

Later, time, once your enemy, becomes a friend.
Slowly, time distances you from the past and leads you into a better future. Time promotes the healing process, gradual at first then gaining speed, and you can feel the movement within you. Soon the days seem a little brighter and the nights are not as long. You find more reasons to smile, only then do you start reshaping your life. Now, with time on your side, you move forward into a new beginning!

The Woman I Loved

If you're lucky, extremely lucky, you'll find that one person in life that makes you burn white hot; that someone who can physically, mentally and emotionally lift you to heights you never imagined. I loved such a woman!

The woman I loved had a spirit that captured the soul of nature itself. She whispered my name like a soft summer breeze, she moved my heart in rotation with that of the earth, she filled my life with all the bounty found on this planet, and all with the warmth of sunshine. In anger the clouds rolled in, and if she was exceedingly angry, it was though a winter storm set over the landscape of our life. For the most part her demeanor was passive and controlled, except for her electric smile which she gave to everyone who earned it. She willingly shared a happy heart and a deep passion for nature's beauty.

The woman I loved was an enigma, a puzzle wrapped in a riddle, and in 29 years I never completely solved her mystery. She had a poet's soul, an artist's eye, and a queen's tastes. A woman born with an infectious laugh and great enthusiasm for living life to it's fullest; one who showed joy in the humanities, and great sorrow in inhumanity. She was unusual in the fact that she never pretended to be more or less than she was, and she expected you to take her for what she was. You needn't pretend in front of her either for she didn't suffer fools or boors well. The woman I loved had a childlike innocence, or at the very least a naiveté, when it came to politics and money; yet she could show the wisdom of Solomon when called upon to defend her use of either.

The woman I loved was a dreamer. Unlike most of us, she never dreamed of enriching her lot in life; her dreams involved enriching the lives of others. She wanted everyone to be happy, to have peace in their life, to be at peace within. And, for the most part, if she dreamed it, wished hard enough for it, it somehow came true to the person she wanted to help. Some of her greatest feats involved straightening the curves and smoothing the bumps in the road of life of others. They, like I, were always amazed when she worked her magic.

The woman I loved lived in much pain near the end. Not always sure of the cause of the pain, she endured it. And when the pain became too intense, she would sit holding her stomach and rock back and forth, and summon all of mental abilities to ward-off the ever-increasing sting of her illness. She was one of the most impressive mental-over-physical practitioners I've ever known, but in the end even her strength was not enough.

The woman I loved died too young!

Warren K. Olson

Turning the Stone

A lifetime reduced to ashes, held in an urn;
non-descript on the surface, but
a biography when the stone is turned.
For among the ashes one can read
a childhood filled with wonder and laughter;
of puppy love, teenage dramatics, proms, and college after.
Swimming, skiing, and the careers that followed,
adventures of a lifetime earned on time owned,
not borrowed.

A life of adult love, given and taken,
times of tension, times of ease.
The story of stepchildren loved and nurtured,
of fulfilling grandparents and parents needs.
A life of friendship and photos,
a life of happiness and tears.
A life filled with all life gives you,
with memories lasting through the years.

And toward the end a life of courage,
fighting against illnesses' march;
a life silhouetted on gray shaded walls,
silhouettes cast by the light of life's torch.
A life read within the ashes,
a lifetime held in an urn
with individual life stories compacted
and relived only in memory
when the stone is turned.

The wise reader knows what lies within the ashes
and sees her lifetime held in an urn;
he'll carry that lifetime and the memories with him
and they will hopefully re-tell the story...
when his stone is turned.

Warren K. Olson

Where Does Love Go

Where does love go when the body has been taken away,
when no one is left to speak the words?
One finds that in time it remains in your mind,
and in all you ever heard.

Love is there; hidden in a verse of a song,
there with each new dawn.
The love you were given stays deep in your soul
and perhaps deeper within your heart,
And that love awakens, making you whole,
even tho' you are apart.

You can find it in a wisp of memory,
in a passing thought or phrase,
and sometimes even when your mind is numb
love glimmers through the haze.
It rises like the morning sun and
helps you through rough days,
and therein lies the beauty of love
for it never goes away.

The secret is to recognize the signs
and throughout each passing day
you will come to know that within your soul,
love has never gone away.
The love you knew is more precious now,
it's meaning more intense,
and the world you both built for two,
suddenly makes more sense.

So look within for the signs of love
and you find it every day;
so where does love go when the body has gone?
It never went away.

Love

A Footprint in Time

Look into my eyes, there you will find the promise of tomorrow.
Look into my heart and you will see room for you there.
Look into my soul and take all you care to borrow,
for those parts of me I most willingly share.

Leave but a commitment to walk with me, to live
and to return, in kind, that which you find.
Use what you will for it is mine to give,
and together we will leave a single footprint in time.

A Lovers Glance

Silent whispers, unspoken words, simply from the glance of a lover.

A slight smile, a knowing look;
a gesture of the mind and
a gesture of the body.

This is a communication meant for only two.

A collective heartbeat, sequential movement
that creates one out of two,

a symphony out of silence...
simply from the glance of a lover.

A Need

There is a need in each of us to love and to be loved,
a yearning that cries out from deep within our soul,
to be a part of love, and hold love high above,
for it's the love that makes us whole.

The need grows as we move through life and struggle to hold tight
each dream, and our wish for more is a natural sight
for our eyes and hearts watch a changing scene.

The need never ends, the want never dies
as we travel along life's journey,
to fulfill what our soul desires....
for its love's promises that holds life's key!

Warren K. Olson

As Love Ends

As silently and swiftly as it entered, love exits,
leaving behind a trail of what might have been.
Now the sun sets behind a masking group of clouds,
signaling the sounds of darkness as love ends.

The once warm breeze becomes a chilling wind,
laughter turns to sorrow.
Two lives abruptly change as love ends
and the pain will last through an endless tomorrow .

The birds are strangely muted now,
flowers have lost their bloom,
and two hearts and minds question how
clear skies could be usurped by gloom.

Yes, heartfelt promises are cast aside
as former lovers pretend to be friends,
as they taste the salt of their tears that have dried
in the lonely silence of life as love ends.

Bring Unto Me

Bring to me your love unencumbered
and I will bring mine to you.
Lives past do not count, days and
years shall stay unnumbered
as we move forward with life anew.

Bring to me your dreams and wishes
and I will take them into my heart;
wishes to grant and dreams to fulfill
as we bask in love's new start.

Bring to me your fears, from childhood on,
for there can be no light without darkness,
and I shall protect you from these shadowed places
by showing you where my heart is.

Bring to me all that you will,
for all will be gifts over time.
Bring to me a heart full of love,
and I will bring you mine.

Christine II

Carrying a basket filled with love

Holding on to its delicate handle

Removing the contents one by one

In the light of a soft glowing candle

Sharing each, she carefully displays

The items the basket holds

In the flame's flickering light

Now the last gift of the night to unfold

Ever so dear, the gift that appears

is the key that unlocks her soul.

Comfort Zone

Two bodies lay together in an early morning sleep,
but within the recesses of a dreaming mind,
each feel the body heat;
and it makes the heart smile to not be all alone,
a sigh escapes through sleeping lips
within the comfort zone.

Early morning coffee, clearing the cobwebs from the mind,
dreams that passed through the night have been left far behind.
But within two hearts rests the feeling, one of being home;
warmth on a chilly morning,…. from the comfort zone.

Throughout the day you see her pass by, chores demand her time,
and you too go about the day, doing your chores in-kind.
The thoughts of *two* play in your mind like verses from a poem,
and a smile crosses your face… a gift from the comfort zone.

Two bodies lay together in early morning sleep,
but within the recesses of a dreaming mind
each feels the body heat.
And it makes the heart smile to not have to stand alone;
and loving spirits soar through the starlit sky
of the comfort zone.

Dancing Shadows

Beautiful eyes that glisten in the candlelit night
showing an emotion meant for only two.
Creating a moment that happens too seldom in life
exchanging knowing glances as lovers do.

Hair resting softly on bare shoulders,
speaking volumes in breathy whispers
the words in ways now bolder
that intrigue the lover-listener.

Soft curves reflecting firelight
with dancing shadows playing with each space;
reclining beauty that captures the heart of the night
and your souls want to stay in this place.

Two lovers holding tight to a feeling
and a love not experienced by most;
a treasured time that sends two hearts reeling
as tonight, and forever, become love's host.

For Chris

She is one of constant movement,
the winds of change blow steadily through her life,
leaving all within that change a blurred confusion,
twisting time and tasks and sometimes
turning day in to night.

Her stress level is constantly pushed to the breaking point
with daily changes it's hard for one to understand,
just what it is within her that allows her
to anoint those changes
as a part of her master plan.

How she survives is a mystery to most who know her,
but she does with rescues that arrive in the nick of time.
If the rescues fail she will surely suffer, and lose all…
with the exception of her mind.

Will or can she slow down,
calm the winds of change that complicate her life?
I'm not sure if she can,
or even cares to;
she's used to changes and
she takes it all in stride.

But as she gets older can she function with her life in turmoil,
will she remain fast enough
to react
"always in time"?
Can she continue to let her life be run by erratic toil,
or will she lose all…
with the exception of her mind?

Her Eyes

Her eyes are a glimmering reflection of her thoughts;
eyes that are the passageway to her soul,
a mirror image of her heart.

The eyes laugh silently in joy,
fill with hushed tears in sadness, and spark in anger.
But always, always, they convey her "being" from within their color.

Eyes that tell a history, that dream of the future.
Eyes that respond to touch and sound,
her eyes speak all that she needs to say.

Her eyes, an intrinsic convergence of muted feelings,
a voiceless communication of the moment.
Yes, her eyes are more than another component of beauty,
they speak all that she needs to say!

I Can't Promise

I can't promise you the moon for it's not mine to give,
and the stars must stay in heaven to fully shine,
but I promise you this life which is mine to live
and I'll give all my love until the end of that time.

I can't promise you diamonds or other fancy things,
and the best of me is all that I can give to you.
I can't promise endless summers or eternal spring,
what I bring is love, a lasting love that's true.

I can't promise that our love will last forever,
or that our love will stand the test of endless time.
What I give to you is my soul for as long as we're together,
and a pledge to treat your heart and soul as if they were both mine.

I can't promise you sunshine each passing day,
for in life there are times when the sky is gray.
What I promise is my heart which will carry you along,
and a life and a love that will be here until I'm gone.

In the Dark of Lace

In the dark of lace in the night, two bodies come together,
each seeking the freedom that sex brings;
a passion of the mind, a passion of the body;
a physical prayer for emotional release.

A silent shout as nerves and muscle involuntarily move,
jumping from sensory to sensory
leaving a quickening of mind and soul;
jolts of kinetic electricity send shockwaves
from body to body.

Temperatures rise, and then create flames in the mind,
skin that becomes increasingly sensitive to touch,
a hidden landscape that begs to be explored,
and nerve endings crying-out for mercy!

The rocking explosion of scorching force,
then rainbow colors traverse the mind;
and moist bodies now cool…
in the dark of lace in the night.

Just as Love Planned

There is light beyond the shadows,
there is hope after shattered dreams,
your heart will beat strong after healing,
the cloak of life may be re-worn
after mending tattered seams.

You will find joy in a child's laughter,
a soft-spoken voice, a gentle touch;
Soon you'll see that it's all that you're after,
after losing all before,
and missing it so much.

There will be beauty in hidden gardens,
ones you missed along the way,
while you were lost the gardens blossomed,
saving their beauty for this day.

When you least expect it love will touch you,
caressing your soul with velvet-gloved hands,
lifting your spirit and letting love guide you
… just as love planned.

Yes, there is light beyond the shadows,
in a soft spoken voice,
in love's caressing hands;
there it will be standing before you
… just as love planned.

One Woman in Time

How did this happen, how did I find such a bright light where once
there was only darkness,
and when did I find the one woman in time
who showed me where my heart is?

Did fate play the guiding role that brought me to this place,
one where serenity lies under starry skies,
as I let my mind drift into her space?

When exactly did the transition occur that lifted my spirit inside,
that awakened my soul,
that now makes me whole,
after I thought those parts had died?

Will I ever know as I watch my love grow
and await new-life's tender kiss;
when did I find the one woman in time…
who showed me where my heart is?

Passions Rise

There is a moist warmth to her body,
a sensuous sweet odor
that captivates my senses
and leaves them reeling.
Skin, soft and tan, that glistens during our private times
and accepts freely my touch and feelings.

Her blonde hair changes style with the night,
first with a formal flair,
then free-flowing in the dark.
It frames her face, although tousled now,
it also frames my heart.

Her passion moves her to increasing heights as a white heat abounds.
It leaves her breathless, muscles convulsing,
a voice of hoarse whispers.
A damp trail of kisses creates a path showing
where passion has been,
then silent prayers to an unseen god as she
recites her own mental vespers.

We both feel it now as her body awakes and
starts trembling in the dark,
involuntary moves that increases the mood
as she floats on passions rise.
When the moment arrives mind and body collide,
a volcanic form of fire,
leaving both to hold on before the moment escapes
into passion's night skies.

Passion's Storm

In the late night our body's alight and come together in passion,
like the skies of a summer storm
when it is the norm
to see the storm
clouds clashing.

Our hands and lips explore worlds never felt before,
and we treasure each stop on our journey.
Our souls are inflamed, not cooled by our storms rain,
as each holds a magical key.

As the intensity grows like searing hot coals,
the only sound is our breathing;
with bodies waiting for the lighting to strike,
the height of anticipation seething.

We continue to explore and silently we implore
that each chooses wisely the path of this storm;
with minds aligned
with the storm's time,
and bodies in
synchronous form.

The storm's crescendo builds toward a towering high,
then the lightening strikes and bodies arch,
as though trying to touch the sky.

After the storm, in a period of calm, two bodies lie together,
wrapped in each others arms,
and safe from all harm,
each praying the next storm lasts forever!

Portrait in Alabaster

Alabaster skin with the slight taste of salt,
breathing slows now as excitement
wanes and muscles relax.

Hair disheveled, arranged by passion's embrace.
A slight smile flirts with the look of contentment,
and eyes are moist with the feelings released moments ago.

One legs drifts over another's, and finds its place;
head nestled against a shoulder as a sigh escapes.
Two hearts rapidly beating as one, as bodies and
minds bask in the warmth of new memories.

A soft voice speaking as a whisper;
words spoken in the moments of passion,
each reciting its own mental vespers.

Promise

Her whisper of promise is like a soft summer breeze,
there is contentment in her voice, that and love.

Speaking in the daylight as well as in the hush of darkness
is a voice resonant with a hint of tomorrow.

The content is inconsequential, it is her presence in the
present, the here and now, which makes the words ring true.

See the Beauty

Truly see the beauty that is inside me,
although I'm flattered by your attentions to the physical,
take the time to enter my heart and mind,
and make our time together mystical.

Weave your dreams and wishes within mine,
let us create a cloak of one;
a love that may last throughout time,
and we'll wrapped the cloak around stars and sun.

Come to me, fears and all,
and I'll do my best to calm;
to protect, to guide, to honor you,
and to keep you from all harm.

Be with me as an equal,
for there shall be no upper hand.
Stay with me as a woman in love,
and take me as your man.

Truly see the beauty in me
for it is the greatest gift I can give,
spend your future life in harmony
for as long as we both shall live.

Rest your soul within mine,
bring your heart in an open hand;
for is my wish to match you fully in-kind
with an inner beauty that will forever stand.

Sensual Song

Her fingers dance across my skin, as soft as a butterfly's wing.

Her mouth searches along my body leaving
the soft, moist trail of her lips;

one leg entwines mine as she continues playing this concerto.

Some how she, through gentle physical movements only,
enters my mind

and whispers her sensual song.

Her tongue darts, leaving each place it touches longing for more;
ever moving,

ever creating new longings.

My muscles are both tense and relaxed, as tho'
confused by the attention, and

a thousand nerve endings explode,
as she whispers her sensual song.

She is both orchestra and conductor
as the symphony of my body is played;

And the chorus sings softly along,
as she whispers her sensual song.

Soft

Soft, is the gentle laying of her hand over yours at dinner.
Soft, is the quick kiss on the cheek she gives.

Soft, is the smoky voice that sings along with
the love songs playing on the radio.
Soft, is the, "Good morning," uttered from beneath warm linens.

Soft, is the sleepy leg entwined in yours, just moments before sleep;
Soft, is the freshly brewed coffee placed before you.

Soft, is the discussion of joint hopes and dreams;
soft is the trust placed in each other.

Hard... is when soft is gone!

Sunday's Woman

The harsh reality of daily life takes its toll on that we covet
our needs are obvious and we come together in a Saturday night fury
to prove we haven't lost it.
The weekend's bring a calming time and clearer sky's prevail, and
Sunday's woman is softer now for she has dropped the veil.
Sunday's woman is one of quiet beauty
and I'm captured by her sleeping body, and
the white-hot sex of the night before
is transformed into pure sensuality.
For she is more open now and speaks in softer tone;
her life and mind have freedom
and she knows she is not alone.
She tenderly touches my arm and smiles, not with just lips but eyes,
Sunday's woman has a warmer heart while under Sunday's skies.
Over coffee and breakfast at a leisurely pace
the past week's storms subside,
and when you gaze into her eyes they have nothing left to hide.
On Sunday I can reach her soul,
feel the warmth she holds inside;
with barriers down vulnerability reigns, and she lets her spirit glide.
Sunday's woman allows her laughter to peak yet
can glow in reflective silence;
she holds on dearly to the end of this week
with it's no makeup, no worry, no bravados to air,
and truly no need for defense.
Sunday's woman is a happier one with her troubles laid to rest,
and of all the women she can become...
I like Sunday's woman the best.

Tapestry

Two small pieces of nearly non-descript cloth,
her colors more bold than his;
his a mottled blend of whites and grays,
not a lot to give.

Her's only somewhat brighter, age has toned the colors down,
has reds, and greens, and blues, tho' soft, the colors do abound.
Separately, the cloths and colors are not much to see;
But when woven together like two souls united,
they become a tapestry!

The Kiss

She leaned forward and kissed me; not soft, not hard...
she just kissed me.
Her right hand touched my neck and she
drew me to her waiting mouth.
Soft lips, slightly parted, lingered, and then
she rested her forehead against mine.
Was this the kiss of a new beginning, or that of goodbye;
a promise of more, or
the thing of soon-to-be history?

Neither of us spoke, we just let the moment last,
with two hearts racing.
She pulled her head back and looked deeply into my eyes.
A small soft smile formed on *those* lips
and she tilted her head and kissed me again;
not hard, not soft... she just kissed me.

This time I kissed back;
not soft,
not hard...
just gently kissed her back.
A natural place of universal comfort, a comfort I had not felt before;
and yet excitement that felt right,
like that of the first romantic kiss of youth.
And time stopped while our lips touched,
the only pendulum was a beating heart,
the only sound a quiet sigh that seemed
to come from deep within her.

My hands, off on their own journey, clumsily found her shoulders,
and the palm of her hand still rested on my neck;
only now directions were not necessary.
My body trembled and my mind was a kaleidoscope of exploding colors;
not bright, not dull… just colors,
some of which I'd never seen before.

Velvet kisses, each containing passive emotion,
each with a promise of not just tonight.
Movements of two, so synchronous that they became one,
and silence that became a choir.
Love could start and grow from this endless moment,
and all because she kissed me;
not soft, not hard…

she just kissed me.

Where Do We Go From Here?
(Dreams and Wishes)

We set the tone early, each expressing what we want… and need.

And each imploring that within our heart,

that our own heart takes heed

to understand what the other dreams and wishes

and matching it to our own

and praying through a growing love

that our dreams will find a home.

     Now ten months in, we again reflect on

     just what was" meant to be",

     changes occur within our life's

     and it's not easy to see

     just what wishes and dreams can do to make this true love last,

     to allow each heart to live within love,

     and not relive the past.

          Sure, but not too sure, if indeed our hearts are strong,

          we ponder the existence of our love,

          and the roads it must travel along.

          Still, the need to assure, to know our love is true,

          Takes time,…….. and time alone;

          for we know inside,

          and above all,

          our dreams and wishes

          need a home!

Whispers

Whispers in the dark, soft whispers, no more than a sigh,
produce subtle thoughts in the night stillness.

Whispers in the dark, bringing two hearts closer,
so close as to create one.

Whispers in the dark, adding to the emotion
and depth of your soul.

Whispers in the dark, drawing two bodies closer to white-hot
and searing passion that burns... even within the mind.

All this and much more initiated by whispers in the dark,
whispers no louder than a sigh.

LaVergne, TN USA
31 December 2009

168673LV00005B/6/P